OFF WE GO!

TO DELHI, TO DELHI

TALKING CUB
Speaking Tiger Publishing Pvt. Ltd
4381/4 Ansari Road, Daryaganj, New Delhi - 110002, India

Published in Talking Cub, an imprint of Speaking Tiger, in association with INTACH in hardback in 2019

ISBN: 978-93-88874-48-9
eISBN: 978-93-88874-49-6

10 9 8 7 6 5 4 3 2 1

Designed by Aniruddha Mukherjee for Syllables27, a specialised children's content outfit run by the authors to produce books for children on a turn-key basis for various publishers and organisations.

Printed at Impressions Printing & Packaging Ltd., Noida

talking CUB | INTACH

OFF WE GO!
TO DELHI, TO DELHI

Written by Arthy Muthanna Singh &
Mamta Nainy
Illustrated by Aniruddha Mukherjee

'DING! We're about to land at the Indira Gandhi International Airport! We've covered the distance of 7672 miles from San Francisco to New Delhi in 16 hours 20 minutes. The temperature outside is 28° Celsius. We wish you a pleasant stay and look forward to welcoming you onboard again!'

Did you hear the Captain's voice over the loudspeaker? We've finally reached Delhi - the tiny dot that I saw on the world map while tracing the route from my home in the US to here. Delhi is where my grandparents, uncles, aunts and cousins live, but guess what, this is my first visit to the city - and I just can't wait to explore it.

FAST FACTS

Before the plane lands, here are some quick facts about Delhi:

Area: 1,484 square kilometres

Population: Hold your breath - 1.9 crore

Commonly Spoken Languages: Hindi, English, Punjabi and Urdu

Destination Delhi!

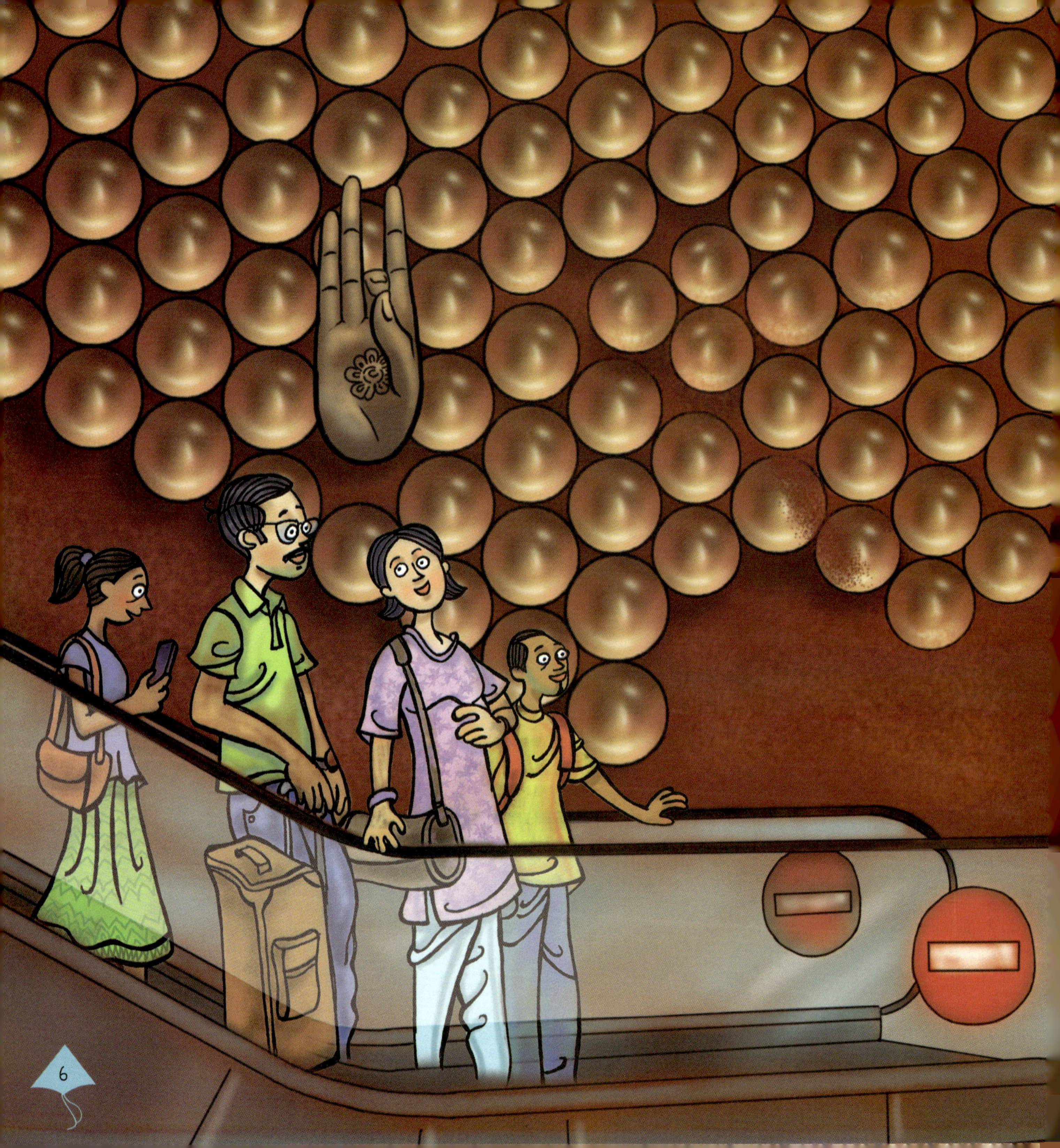

The board says it's Terminal 3 of the airport, but it looks like a magic maze to me. It has so many travellers, all in a hurry. I wonder where they're all off to.

Wow - look there! Do you see those nine giant metallic hands waving at us? Papa tells me that these are called *mudras* or hand gestures and they are a part of the traditional Indian dance forms.

BUSY AS A BEE

Do you know that Terminal 3 of the IGI airport is the 25th busiest airport in the world with a passenger capacity of 34 million per year? Now that's really a lot!

INDIRA GANDHI IN
AIRPORT

Outside the airport, apart from Maama, Maami and my cousin Rinku, a blast of hot air welcomes us. Phew! I never expected Delhi to be this hot.

We load our baggage into the car and get on the road. It has vehicles of all colours, shapes and sizes – big and small cars and multi-coloured buses. But I have never seen autorickshaws before, and so many zooming scooters.

As we drive past many buildings, they all seem jumbled up and very close together. Rinku tells me her teacher told her that Delhi is the world's second most populated city, just after Tokyo in Japan.

After a rather long drive, we enter a place that looks straight out of the stories in the *Arabian Nights*! It has narrow alleys, ancient-looking houses, small shops, street vendors, cycle rickshaws, half-awake dogs, fat goats and lazy cows.

'This is the old part of Delhi,' says Maama. 'Our house is just round the corner.'

'You know, Tiya,' says Rinku, 'Delhi is very, very old!'

'How old? Older than dinosaurs?' I ask.

'No,' she says, smiling. 'But still very old. It's been there since the time of the Mahabharata. It was called Indraprastha at that time.'

'But how did it become Delhi then?' I ask.

'There are many stories about it,' Maama tells me. 'One of them says that it came from the Urdu word *dehaleez*, meaning "entrance", for it was the entry point to the Indo-Gangetic plains. Another one says that long ago there was a Mauryan king named Raja Dhilu. He built this city and named it after himself. A third story says that Delhi was once the kingdom of a weak ruler and it was called *dhila*, (Hindi for loose), from where the name "Delhi" came.'

But which one of these stories is actually true? Maama doesn't know. Do you?

स. हरप्रीत सिंह नू
गुरुद्वारा शीशगंज साहिब दे
दी सेवा देन लई
दा धन्यवाद

'Ta-Da! We are home!' Maama announces as he stops the car in front of an old house with faded blue walls. The paint on the walls is peeling off, making them look like the Pacific Ocean with small islands in between.

Naniji and Nanaji rush out to meet us. They both hug me tight. I see Naniji wiping tiny drops of tears from her eyes with the edge of her dupatta.

The house is huge. 'It has eleven rooms and five terraces,' Rinku tells me as we climb up the stairs – the marble of which is chipped at places.

'Five terraces? How nice!' I exclaim. 'I only have one in my home, that too five floors above our house.'

After dinner and much talk, I change into my nightclothes and even before I get into bed – *Khurr...Phisss...Khurr...Phiss...*I'm snoring.

HERITAGE HAVELIS

Old Delhi has many old havelis or mansions – some of them dating back to the Mughal era. They have huge doorways, marble arches and beautiful windows. Did you know Old Delhi also has the haveli of the famous poet Mirza Ghalib?

Desi Kitchen

Rinku is up early next morning. 'Let's have breakfast and go to the terrace!' She shakes me awake while I'm still rubbing sleep off my eyes.

On the terrace, Rinku shows me how to fly kites. It's so much fun! I watch as she brings down someone's kite so easily. A kite fight!

'What's that?' I ask, pointing at a big dome in the distance.

'That's Jama Masjid,' Rinku tells me. 'The biggest mosque in India. Don't the tall pillars around the mosque look like they're praying to the skies?'

They do!

I can happily spend the whole day here, staring at the vast sky with multi-coloured kites floating in it like small dragonflies.

But, that's not to be. Maami calls us for lunch. She makes such yummy food that Rinku and I are happy to delay the kite flying.

जलेबी

That evening, we go to a market in Chandni Chowk. Seated in a rickety rickshaw, we make our way through the busy by-lanes of Old Delhi.

'Why is it called Chandni Chowk?' I ask Rinku, but the rickshaw-walla answers instead.

'I'll tell you, *bitiya,*' he says. 'Hundreds of years ago, the Mughal Emperor Shah Jahan built Old Delhi and named it Shahjahanabad. He also created a beautiful market so that his daughter Jahanara – who designed the market – did not have to go far away to shop. The Yamuna River used to flow from the centre of the market. And on full-moon nights, it reflected the moonlight. So this market was named Chandni Chowk or the Moonlit Square.'

'Isn't it the same Shah Jahan who built the famous Taj Mahal in Agra?' I whisper into Rinku's ears. I do not want the rickshaw-walla to think I do not know anything.

'Yes,' Rinku says. 'He also built the Red Fort, a fort named after the red walls around it, and Jama Masjid – the mosque that we saw from the terrace.'

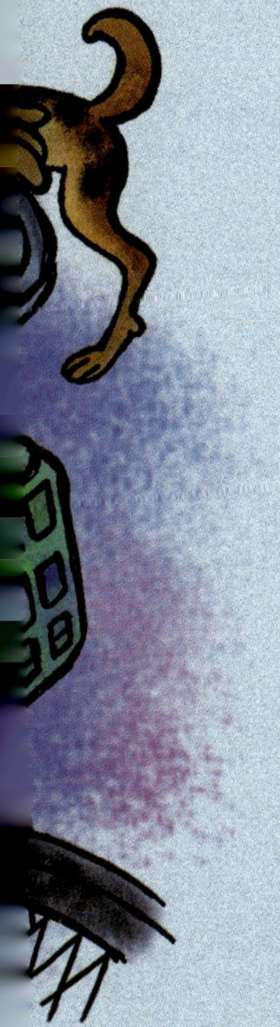

THE SEVEN CITIES OF DELHI

Did you know that Delhi once had seven cities within it? Kings from different dynasties chose a part of Delhi and made it their capital city. These cities were Qila Rai Pithora, Mehrauli, Siri, Tughlaqabad, Ferozabad, Shergarh and Shahjahanabad. Imagine so many cities within a city!

We get off our rickshaws just outside a shop selling puffy *golgappas.* Maami says there's also a Paranthewali Gali close by that has shops that sell the most unusual *parathas* – even one with the stuffing of bitter gourd. That surely doesn't sound too tasty though!

After having a lot of spicy and crunchy *golgappas,* we decide to go back home. But then, a delicious aroma draws us to a roadside stall selling hot *samosas...*

WHEN IN OLD DELHI...

1. Gobble up *dahi-bhallas* and *tikkis* at Natraj Dahi Bhalle.
2. Try *poori-bhaji, kachori-subzi* and *daulat ki chaat.*
3. And the syrup-dripping *jalebis* at the Famous Jalebi Wala.
4. Do not miss the *matka kulfi* that many Old Delhi shops sell.

Mangu Ke
Samose

Guess where we go the next day? Here's a hint: It's the world's tallest brick minaret – at least that's what Rinku tells me.

The Qutb Minar!

Maama parks his car next to a big board that says 'Qutb complex'.

'Why complex?' I ask.

'That's because apart from the main minaret, this place has many other monuments too,' he replies.

We enter the complex and head towards the Qutb Minar. It's a tall, TALL minaret. 'Isn't it fabulous?' asks Rinku. I crane my neck to look at it till I get a crick...Owww...Owww!

'The Qutb Minar was built by the Delhi Sultan Qutb-ud-din Aibak in 1192 to mark the victory of Mohammad Ghori over the Rajput King Prithviraj Chauhan,' Mummy reads from an information board next to the Minar.

PILLAR HUGGING!

The Qutb Minar complex also has an iron pillar. The guide says that all your wishes can come true if you hug this pillar. But now there's a fence around it. (Guess the pillar was fed up of people's love!)

Ahrrmmm...ahrmmm...Rinku clears her throat and says, 'Can I add more?'

I nod.

'But Aibak only completed the first level of this minar. Sadly, he fell down from his horse while playing polo and died. The rulers who followed him added various levels to it. It's 72 metres high, has five storeys and 379 stairs. Earlier people were allowed to climb the tower, but not anymore!'

Rinku knows quite a lot of history, I decide.

'And what's that tower with the broken edges?' I ask her, looking at a tower close to Qutb Minar that looks unfinished.

'That's Alai Minar. Sultan Allauddin, who began to build it, wanted to build a tower that was double the height of Qutb Minar, but strangely he too died before it could be finished.'

'Double the height of Qutb Minar!' I wonder. 'It would have surely touched the moon then.'

Just then, Rinku sees a man with a wicker basket on his head and a wooden tripod under his arm. 'Let's have *shakarkandi*,' she says.

'What's that?' I ask.

Rinku then makes me taste the spiciest sweet potatoes I've ever had!

MONUMENT MARVEL

Apart from Qutb Minar, Delhi has many other beautiful monuments. If you're a history buff just like Rinku and me, you can:

1. Enjoy a boat ride at the Old Fort.
2. Take a walk at Humayun's Tomb, built in the memory of the Mughal king Humayun. Just a little distance away from the tomb is Nizammudin Dargah, the shrine of the famous Sufi-saint Nizamuddin Auliya.
3. See the stars at Jantar Mantar, one of the best astronomical observatories built by Maharaja Jai Singh in 1725.
4. Visit Mehrauli Archaeological Park that has about 100 monuments that will show you 1000 years of Delhi's history!

PHOOLWALON
KI
SAIR

We come out of the Qutb Minar complex and I see a group of people carrying huge fans in their hands. No, not like the one that's there in Naniji's room and makes a racket with its whirr...whirr...but fans made of beautiful flowers.

'Look at that!' I almost jump in my seat, 'such big flower fans!'

'Oh yes,' says Maami. 'That's Phoolwalon Ki Sair.'

'Phoo...what?!'

'Phool-walon-ki-sair, which means flower-bearers on a stroll. It's a week-long festival during which many flower-vendors offer huge flower fans to the holy shrine of the Sufi-saint Khwaja Bakhtiyar Kaki and at the Hindu temple of Lord Krishna's sister Jog Maya in Mehrauli.'

'Why?' I ask.

'Well, therein lies a story,' Maami says.

I listen very carefully as Maami continues. 'The festival first began when Mughal Emperor Akbar Shah II was the ruler of Delhi. The British had also arrived by then and had a strong footing in Delhi. The emperor's younger son Mirza Jahangir did not like the ways of the British. He was so unhappy with them that he insulted a British representative and was immediately arrested by him.'

'And then?' I ask, very excited.

'Then, Mirza's mother promised to walk barefoot to the shrine of Saint Bakhtiyar Kaki as soon as her son was free. Mirza was freed after two years. So the queen decided to visit the shrine. On that day, all the flower-sellers of the city covered the way to the shrine with flower petals and asked her to offer a flower fan at the Jog Maya temple next to the shrine. People believe the festival started from that day.'

'That's an interesting story!' I say.

FUN'TASTIC FESTIVALS!

Many festivals such as Diwali, Holi, Lohri, Id and Christmas are celebrated in Delhi. But Rinku's favourite is Dusshera. She says she loves going to the Ramlila Maidan to see grandly dressed actors perform the Ramayana – especially the ten-headed Ravana!

After Qutb Minar, we go to Lodhi Garden.

'I've never seen a garden so big,' I exclaim as we enter the huge lawns.

'That's because it was made after clearing two big villages,' Papa says. 'During the British rule in India, a British official made this huge garden for his wife, Lady Willingdon, so that she would not miss her home in England very much.'

A WALK THROUGH TIME AND TOMBS

Spread over a sprawling 90 acres, Lodhi Garden features four big monuments: Tomb of Mohammed Shah, Tomb of Sikandar Lodi, Shisha Gumbad, and Bara Gumbad.

'And what are those big structures?' I ask, pointing at some buildings that look very, very old.

'Oh, those!' says Rinku. 'Those are monuments from a very long time ago – from the time of the Sayyid and Lodi kings who ruled Delhi in the 15th century.'

We all play dumb charades and have sandwiches that we have carried from home. Rinku and I also watch the ducks near the pond. Butterflies flit about us and birds sing beautiful songs.

Suddenly she runs off. 'Catch me if you can!' she shouts. I run after her...

After our game of run-and-catch, Rinku tells me that Delhi has many other gardens as well – she has been to each one of them! Have you?

1. Nehru Park
2. Deer Park
3. Japanese Park
4. Buddha Garden
5. Mehrauli Archaeological Park
6. Mahatma Gandhi Park
7. Yamuna Biodiversity Park
8. National Rose Garden

Before we head home, Maama takes us to Dilli Haat. It's a craft and food bazaar which has stalls that house handicrafts from all across India. Food too!

We see some painters making some colourful paintings of fish and peacocks.

'These are Madhubani paintings,' Maami tells me. 'A speciality of Bihar's Madhubani district.'

I wish I could paint like these artists.

Rinku and I watch the puppet show at Dilli Haat. We also get our hair braided.

And then we all finish off with a yummy snack of momos and thukpa from the Sikkim stall.

The next day we decide to give Maama's car some rest, and take the metro instead.

'Where are we going today?' I ask Rinku.

'New Delhi!' she says.

'But didn't you tell me that Delhi is very old? How can it be "new" then?' I ask.

'Delhi is actually made up of two Delhis – Old Delhi and New Delhi,' she says. 'Old Delhi is the more historic part of Delhi which goes back to the times of the Mughals. And New Delhi was designed by the British when they ruled our country.'

'You know, Tiya,' Maama adds, 'Delhi was not always the capital of India. The British shifted their capital from Calcutta to Delhi in 1911. They rebuilt a part of Delhi and added a lot of buildings, offices and markets to it. This part is now called New Delhi.'

It's my first metro ride, and I'm very excited! Papa shows me how to punch in the token at the gate for its flaps to open. As we wait on the platform, the metro comes. The doors open automatically and we enter a coach.

When the lady on the loudspeaker announces our destination, we get off the metro.

We come out of the metro station and take an autorickshaw. The auto takes us on a really broad street, and I see this beautiful palace from far away. I wonder whose it is...

'Palace? Oh no!' says Maama. 'That's Rashtrapati Bhawan – the home of the President of India. This is where the President of India eats, sleeps and runs the country -- not all at once though! It took 17 years to complete. Do you know how many rooms there are in this huge mansion? Over three hundred!'

'Three hundred! It must have taken the President so many days to see all the rooms in his own house,' I think to myself.

WHO BUILT IT?

Rashtrapati Bhawan was designed by the British architect Edwin Lutyens. Before India's Independence, it was the house of the British viceroy who's said to have employed 418 gardeners just to take care of its beautiful gardens. Now called the Mughal Gardens, you can visit them from the first week of February to the second week of March, when they're open to the public.

A little distance away from Rashtrapati Bhawan, we stop at a huge monument. It's surrounded by lawns on all sides.

'This is India Gate,' Rinku says. 'It's actually a war memorial which was built in 1931 to pay tribute to the soldiers who died while fighting in World War I. Their names are on this structure. Under its big arch, burns the Amar Jawan Jyoti. That fire keeps burning always. Can you see the rifle with a soldier's helmet placed on it? Every year, on 26th January, the Republic Day parade happens here and it is very exciting to see the army tanks, fighter planes, and floats from all the states.'

Maama buys us ice-lollies. Licking them, and with our tongues bright orange, we walk down to the Children's Park. There are so many kinds of swings, see-saws and slides in the park. It has a musical fountain and an aquarium, too.

Rinku and I take turns on the swing and play ball till the last rays of the sun turn into light orange...

'Are you hungry?' Maama asks Rinku and me.

We really really are!

'Let's have a snack at the best bakery in town,' he says.

We all go to Wenger's in Connaught Place. It's super crowded. As we wait in the queue, a thick wooden door swings open, and a uniformed man comes out carrying trays of pastries, patties, cookies and chocolates! Yummy!

'Which one would you like to have?' Maama asks me.

'Ummm...that one, that one, that one and that one...'

We come out of the shop, only after we just cannot eat any more!

We walk a long way on the broad, busy corridors of Connaught Place. There are shops of all kinds, restaurants, cafes, cinemas and offices.

'Connaught Place too was born during the times of the British,' Rinku says, she had read somewhere, 'because the British wanted a nice complex for shopping and entertainment. And you won't believe! It was designed in the shape of a huge horse-shoe, for they thought it would be lucky.'

Looking at all the people buying things, eating and enjoying themselves in Connaught Place, I guess they were right!

PSST!

Connaught Place was designed by Robert Tor Russell in 1929. It's named after the Duke of Connaught, a member of the British royal family.

'What's the plan today?' Papa asks us the next morning.

'Today is the museum day,' Rinku announces.

I love going to museums! They are filled with magic and mystery, and they always have so much to discover.

The first museum that we go to is Shankar's International Dolls Museum. And we don't go there by car. No, not even by metro! We take the HOHO bus! It's the funkiest way to explore Delhi. These Hop-On-Hop-Off buses glide around the city and touch all the major tourist spots.

I thought I loved dolls, but when we reach the dolls museum, I realize there was someone who loved dolls even more than I do. Set up by K Shankar Pillai, the dolls museum has about 6500 dolls from 85 different countries. A guard there tells us that Mr Pillai once received a doll from Hungary as a gift which made him start this museum. I also have about 23 dolls. Can I start a museum?

We go to a museum full of trains next. It's the National Rail Museum with very many rare steam trains. Rinku and I pretend to be engine drivers as we climb into the engines!

Rinku says there is also a Toilet Museum in Delhi. It has cushioned toilets, throne-cum-commode and many strange things. It must be the world's weirdest museum.

There are many other museums in Delhi as well:

1. National Museum
2. Gandhi Museum
3. National Science Centre
4. Nehru Memorial Museum and Library
5. Metro Museum

Early the next day, we visit a temple. Nanaji and Naniji also come along. But when we reach there, I find that it doesn't look like a temple at all. It looks like a giant lotus floating on water!

We remove our shoes and go inside the prayer hall. 'Who made such a beautiful lotus?' I ask Rinku.

'Shhh!' she says. 'You have to be really quiet here.'

When we come out, she tells me that this famous temple of the Baha'i faith was designed by an Iranian-Canadian architect named Fariburz Sahba. It took 10 years to build. And the most amazing thing about this temple is that it has no pillars.

'No pillars? But then what does this huge temple stand on?' I ask.

'Some secrets,' she says, 'are not easy to find out!'

PICTURE PERFECT

The Lotus Temple has 27 freestanding petals made of marble. What's more? The marble was flown in from Greece!

While on our way back home, we visit Gurudwara Bangla Sahib. And we enjoy the delicious *langar* of puffy *rotis* and *dal* and the yummy *halwa prasad.*

Next to the gurudwara, I see the Sacred Heart Cathedral. We walk inside and see a wedding taking place. What a lovely white gown the bride was wearing!

My holidays in Delhi are coming to an end. Tomorrow we leave for my Dadaji and Dadiji's home in Lucknow. But before we drive back to Nanaji and Naniji's house, Rinku shows me one last thing. Next to the Sacred Heart Cathedral, there's a round building. She says it has the General Post Office inside. I ask Maama to stop there. I get down, buy a post-card, and drop it in the letter box.

प्रधान डाकघर नई दिल्ली
G.P.O. NEW DEL
I had a great time in Delhi.
I hope you come to Delhi
one day and love it as
much as I did!
To
You, my dear friend
LETTERS
भारतीय डाक
India Post

10 things to eat

1. Chaat
2. Tikki
3. Samosas
4. Kachori
5. Chole-bhature
6. Matar-kulcha
7. Aloo-poori
8. Dahi-bhalle
9. Jalebis
10. Matka Kulfi

THE CAPITAL CITY

Delhi, officially called the National Capital Region, is a city and a Union Territory of India. It includes the country's capital New Delhi.

Rinku says that Delhi is the heart of India. With so many people of varied cultures, religions and beliefs living together in this city, I guess she's right!

10 things to do

1. Go on a picnic in Nehru Park
2. Take a sight-seeing ride on a HOHO (Hop-On-Hop-Off) bus
3. Observe the animals at the zoo
4. Take a boat ride at Purana Qila
5. Understand the workings of the Jantar-Mantar
6. Visit the Children's Museum at Bal Bhavan
7. Look for deer in Deer Park
8. Have an ice cream at India Gate
9. Chill out at the Children's Park
10. Get crafty at the Crafts Museum

10 things to see

1. Nehru Planetarium
2. Dilli Haat
3. Humayun's Tomb
4. Nizamuddin Dargah
5. Rail Museum
6. National Gallery of Modern Art
7. Mehrauli Archaeological Park
8. Adventure Island
9. National Gandhi Museum
10. Red Fort

GLOSSARY

Bitiya: Daughter

Dadaji: Paternal grandfather

Dadiji: Paternal grandmother

Halwa: An Indian dessert

Langar: A community kitchen

Maama: Uncle; mother's brother

Maami: Aunt; wife of mother's brother

Momos: Tibetan dumplings

Mudras: A symbolic hand gesture used in Indian classical dance

Nanaji: Maternal grandfather

Naniji: Maternal grandmother

Prasad: A devotional offering made to a god

Shakarkandi: Sweet potato

Thukpa: Tibetan noodle soup

About Indian National Trust for Art and Cultural Heritage (INTACH)

INTACH is a nationwide, non-profit membership organization to protect and conserve India's vast natural and cultural heritage. It is today the largest organization in the country dedicated to conservation. Heritage Education and Communication Service (HECS) of INTACH spreads awareness about India's natural, built, cultural, and living heritage. HECS promotes a love for heritage amongst children. It runs a network of heritage clubs. Each heritage club works on promoting the local culture and appreciating the rich diversity of India's heritage.

For further details, log on to: www.intach.org, www.youngintach.org

About Talking Cub

Talking Cub is the children's imprint of Speaking Tiger. Launched in December 2017, the imprint has published over thirty-five books, including those by renowned authors such as Ruskin Bond, Paro Anand, Ranjit Lal, Subhadra Sen Gupta, Deepa Agarwal and others. Some of the country's best fiction and non-fiction writing for children is part of the imprint. The details of all the titles can be seen at www.speakingtigerbooks.com.

Arthy Muthanna Singh is a children's writer, freelance journalist, copywriter, editor and cartoonist. She has a diverse range of experience in the publishing industry, a large part of it spent at *Limca Book of Records.* She has authored over thirty-five books for children. She conducts creative writing workshops and dreams of moving to Goa some day.

Mamta Nainy is a children's writer based in New Delhi. She spent some years in advertising before an apple fell on her head while she was sitting under a mango tree, and she had her Eureka moment. She has been writing for children since then. She loves travelling but when she's too lazy to do it, she makes do with reading. She can usually be spotted next to a pile of children's books, chuckling to herself!

An MFA from Delhi School of Art, **Aniruddha Mukherjee** doodles non-stop, photographs riversides, and can usually be spotted next to a pile of children's books. He's illustrated a number of books for children. His works move from the figurative to the fantastical, and use a variety of media from paint to print. Apart from illustrating books for children - which he enjoys the most - he's also worked on other projects, including painting, digital assemblages, murals and wallscapes. His works have been honoured with a number of national and international recognitions.